Advance Praise for *Red Low Fog / Trans*

"An innovative compound of voices, genres, and poetic forms, *Red Low Fog/Transcript* explores the artist's power to transmute harrowing experience into imaginative realms of iridescent but precarious beauty. As readers, we are placed within a community of witnesses struggling to understand how the synergistic collaboration between children's book authors Thomas and Delphine has devolved into enmeshment, psychosis, and even abuse. The intricate framing and use of poetic form is handled with delicacy and fractal purity, allowing multiple narratives to emerge as if in a faceted mirror. Through the fractured enchantment of Thomas and Delphine, Jordan captures the cast's disturbed reflections, the uncertain stability of their own minds and intimate relationships, their secrets hidden in plain sight. An admirable, haunting work of verse—I know of nothing remotely like it."

—Karen Holmberg, author of *The Perseids* and *Axis Mundi*

"*Red Low Fog / Transcript* is a carefully crafted and imaginative collection of poems, many of them written in a variety of traditional forms, all of which combine to provide a detailed view into a world in which nothing is as it seems."

—Roderick Bates, editor, *Rat's Ass Review*

"Q: What do you get when you mix *Fargo*, Shirley Jackson, Harper Valley PTA, Joan Jett & The Runaways, *The Twilight Zone*, and the early recordings of Maybelle & Sara Carter?

A: Melissa E. Jordan's debut poetry collection, *Red Low Fog / Transcript*.

Jordan tells the story of a bombing at a ski lodge in upstate New York, which is entwined with the love story of Thomas Kearne (who is a suspect in the bombing) and his wife, Delphine Kearne (whereabouts unknown). Drawing on the traditions of urban myth, documentary, fairy-tale, small-town gossip, folklore, and reality TV, Jordan leads us through multiple twists & layers of intrigue and mystery. Add to this that the story is narrated by a cast of characters each 'assigned' their own poetic form (villanelle, erasure, ekphrasis, sedoka, etc.) – and this is one of the most unique and inventive collections I've ever read.

Red Low Fog / Transcript will challenge everything you thought you knew about the intersection of poetry, narrative, reality, art, and truth. Jordan has created a true artifact of Americana that will keep you turning the pages at 2 am, without sacrificing one iota of poetic craft. And dear reader, just when you think you know what 'really happened,' I promise that you do not!"

—Beth Gordon, author of
This Small Machine of Prayer and *The Water Cycle*

red low fog
/transcript

[documentary in poems]

melissa e. jordan

Jordan, Melissa E. / author

Red Low Fog/Transcript / Melissa E. Jordan

Poems

ISBN: 978-1-7365167-9-9

Edited by: Amanda McLeod
Book Design: Amanda McLeod
Cover Art: Lucas Favre and Dave Hoefler via Unsplash
Cover Design: Amanda McLeod

PUBLISHER
Animal Heart Press
P.O. Box 322
Thetford Center, Vermont 05075
www.animalheartpress.net

For my mother,
Pamela Lithgow Briggs,
who has graced me with her fierce, unwavering support
from the very beginning.

TRANSCRIPT LOG

Interview Subject	Field Notes	

Part Two

Appearing on the RLF transcript:

Alex Baeza, RLF Director/ Narrator
Blank verse

Birget Møller-Baeza, RLF Editor/VO
Free verse

Delphine Kearne, Children's book author
Villanelle

Thomas Kearne, Children's book illustrator
Anaphora

Kearne joint interviews
Sedoka

Harry Ange, Book editor/mentor
Ottava rima

Lake Tanager Community
Found Poetry

The work of Delphine and Thomas Kearne
Ekphrasis

Additional witness statements
Catena rondo

Adirondack Community Looks for Answers

January 17, 1979

Lake Tanager, NY — Residents of this normally peaceful town are still reeling from the fallout of last Wednesday's bombing at Mount Macron Ski Lodge.

While no one was hurt in the **overnight** attack, the entire ski lift apparatus was destroyed, and two nearby outbuildings damaged, confirmed Mayor Peter Byre.

It is believed that Thomas Kearne, the 27-year-old lifelong resident of Lake Tanager, was behind the bombing. He is currently undergoing psychiatric evaluation, according to his attorney.

"We will be arguing that Thomas' mental state at the time of his action, and which he currently suffers from, would make state prison cruel and unusual punishment," Attorney Dana Golzar noted.

Officials are remaining tight-lipped about what role, if any, Thomas Kearne's wife may have had in the attack. "At this point, **our** understanding is that Mrs. Kearne was not in town when the bomb was placed. Beyond that, we are still pursuing our **own** investigation," said Byre.

Local residents said the young couple were **reserved** but well-liked members of Lake Tanager. Thomas Kearne is a native of the Adirondack town — even moving, in recent years, to a **parcel of** land on the legendary Kearne family "great camp" established in the early 1900s.

Thomas and Delphine Kearne have become local celebrities in the last few years following the publications of several well-received books for young readers, published by Hearts **ease &** Rue Press in Glens Falls.

Delphine Kearne, 25, is believed to have left town several days before the events of last Wednesday. Residents say that they were unclear about where she might have gone.

"I think she's from one of those Carolina islands and used to have a different name," said Sabrina Lewis, a waitress at the town's Star Diner. "I also heard she was emancipated or ran away or something, and moved to our area just a few years back."

Alex Baeza, a filmmaker based in Marfa, TX, said that he had interviewed the couple several times for a planned documentary, part of a series on artistic couples that he and his wife, editor Birget Møller-Baeza, have created for PBS.

"We're just in shock," said Baeza. "This has been our most **treasured** project yet because of the way they work together and the way they just *are* together, and the **faith** they have **in** each other's talents.

"We didn't have any real idea that anything was wrong, although the last time we filmed he...well, it's just hard to know sometimes if things really are quite as **steady** as they seem."

Baeza said that he and Møller-Baeza had been close to finishing their documentary on the couple when they heard about the incident.

"We were already debating about the title, about whether calling it 'Ribbon of Light' was too cheesy. That's something from one of their books, and Delphine had talked movingly about how the **grace** of working together, and just their whole life together, really, felt like stepping up from the rubble onto this ribbon of light, so they'd made a fairytale about it.

"We're just really worried about why Delphine **vanished** this time," added Baeza.

Asked what he meant by 'this time,' Baeza said that he'd shared with police information recorded in an interview for the documentary. "She talked, for what would have been the first time publicly, about how she had been a teen runaway who'd previously endured the foster care system – but could not face going back to her home after her mother remarried immediately upon leaving prison.

"She gave us the impression that she just took off into the night in a station wagon seven or eight years ago-- this young kid," Baeza said. "The most she ever said on record about how she got away was, 'I had my reasons and I had my angels.'"

Each breath was taken in pure collaboration
(that's how we branded ourselves to the world),
life and art tapping out sweet syncopation.

Maybe all I want now is simple ablation,
scraping more of his memory with every charge hurled.
Each breath was taken in pure collaboration.

The legal "collaborate" — now, *there's* a new connotation,
like a showman's prized cane grown all twisted and burled;
life and art tapping in sick syncopation.

Face it: I collaborated in my own annihilation,
sailing right over the brink with my banner unfurled.
Each breath was taken in pure collaboration.

And still (*Write* it!) without him there's no joy in creation,
no fearless dive fathoms-downward for pearls,
life and art tapping out sweet syncopation.

Sometimes in dreams there's a golden way station;
a space we've carved out for sweet assignation.
Each breath is taken in pure collaboration,
life and art tapping out sweet syncopation.

Part One

The pine-tree dreameth of the palm,
And the palm-tree yearns for the pine.
--Henriech Heine

Alex Baeza

When the Jeep hits midpoint on the
sloped drive, cat's ears begin to rise –
slo-mo reveal of twin A-frames,
the cabins stitched together by
a blunt low shed, mullein-windowed.
We're meeting the fourth pair in our
series on artistic couples.
(First was the Provincetown sculptor
and his Welsh partner, a potter,
working clubbily inside their
glass studio over the dunes.
Next, the elderly married Maine
poets – each one celebrated,
and each one already writing
elegiacally about the
other; we filmed them walking the
gentle slopes behind their white barn,
intoning all their best-known works.
And most recent, the Slab City
empty-nesters chaotically
strewing their gallery garden
with welded pieces foraged from
weeks-long trips to the high desert
in a green overlander rig,
searching for downed saguaro ribs
and rusted-out pickup frames.)
On this bright cold Adirondack
morning we'll be interviewing
the youngest-ever Caldecott
nominees, a husband and wife
with a half-dozen picture books
already bringing them acclaim.
She writes and he illustrates but
they insistently describe a
more seamless collaboration,
a true marriage of ink and paint.
On each of their books' front covers
their names are interconnected

with snaking Tasha Tudor vines,
the "s" in Thomas arching back
to grip in its leafy tendrils
the thin spine fronting Delphine's name.
I'm unloading some gear from the
cargo box and Birget's checking
her log notes when both cabin doors,
each within its own triangle,
open simultaneously, and
a willowy shape emerges
from each, like something out of a
fairytale, or Bavarian clock.
And, like children trapped inside those
brutish black forests, we all freeze
for a few startled beats, then stir
sheepishly as we finally
move forward, the work slithering
unseen from our eight outstretched hands.

Harry Ange

I don't think I could ever *quite* get across
their flow back and forth, like two ribbony chains –
or this sand art thing – Watch both waves break and toss:
Each crest – rose or teal – stretches fingers of grain,
clasping in margins when the center gets lost.
See how this shifting double helix remains –
even as the frame itself judders and turns?
… Best I can tell you about knowing the Kearnes.

Witness statement: Daniel Hill, stepfather of Delphine Kearne

You might as well just use her real name.
OK, so I wouldn't want to speak out of turn,
but she was born Darcy — "the dark one," you'll learn.
You might as well just use her real name.

Joint interview: Delphine Kearne and Thomas Kearne

DK   light fell down in shards
on fifth-wheels under live oaks;
hanging moss cast lacy shade

TK   snow blurred the green steel
that stretched first across the gorge,
then climbed beside frozen falls

⌣

DK   before the sun set,
metal roofs at the crossroads
blazed orange, then dulled with night

TK   roadside trading posts,
doors stained picnic-table red,
slumped behind split-rail fences

⌣

DK   rip-rap guarded docks;
as the marsh tides rose higher,
redfish swarmed to feed on crabs

TK   a long wooden rack
held seven orderly rows
of fresh green Kevlar canoes

DK   flat granite new-etched;
red and pink camellias screened
kneeling figures planting bulbs

TK   a three-walled cabin
braced by branching cedar logs
sheltered a fieldstone oven

⌒

DK   a dashboard, faded
to ashes-of-roses, held
one twisted cigarette pack

TK   bathing suits hung from
a slotted grandfather clock
standing on a cracked slate floor

⌒

DK   the woman drove home;
opened her truck door, then sat
staring out the grimed windshield

TK   a pine bough was breached;
the hood of the car veered left
onto a road marked Private

Witness statement: Li Tianshe, teacher at Grantville School

I would not wish to speak out of turn,
but that girl deserved better than what she got.
The smartest thing she did was run away from that lot.
But I would not wish to speak out of turn.

Police Searching for Missing Grantville School Student

May 3, 1971

Greenman, SC — Police are seeking help from the community **in** locating a missing teen girl who is believed to have run away from **her** home at 7585 State Road, **Red** Tin.

Darcy Megget, 17, is described as having long curly brown hair and gray eyes, and is about 5'5" tall. She was last seen wearing her Grantville School uniform – a yellow polo shirt and green plaid skirt.

Local police fear she may have already left the **Low** Country. One witness saw her driving a wood-paneled station wagon in North Charleston. The witness said the evening **fog** prevented her from being sure, but that the vehicle looked similar to one owned by a Grantville School teacher.

But that teacher, Li Tianshe, was unable to offer more information, **she** insisted when reached for comment this morning. Li added that while she was anxious to help authorities, she had already **searched** some of **her** own outbuildings.

"I used it for farm chores and can't really bring to **mind** when it was last used, or what **for**," she said. Li added that she didn't know if she would file **a** stolen car report.

"We don't really know what happened with all that," stepfather Daniel Hill said of the rumor about Darcy being helped out of town, or whether leaving home was even done willingly.

Until last month, Megget had been living in a **Beacon** Island foster home following her mother's arrest for possession of controlled substances last year, and by her grandfather's death shortly after.

Now her family is wondering if Megget's time there may present a clue, according to Hill.

"Maybe she was running with a bad crowd while they had her in foster [care]," her stepfather said. "I told the police to look at that angle, but I don't know."

Delphine Kearne

I had no choice but to build a cabin
from nesting boxes and blue milk crates,
there in the bed of a woody wagon.

I laid down every blanket I could drag in
but left my school clothes to the fates.
I had no choice but to build a cabin.

 I chinked the crates with flannel-back satin —
scrap bin bounties from some lower state —
there in the bed of a woody wagon.

In one tipped crate I set a pewter flagon,
then a specked bowl and a green-rimmed plate.
I had no choice but to build a cabin.

In this tiny space I was the new Aladdin,
pillowed time out of mind, snacking on dates,
there in the bed of a woody wagon.

Some nesting boxes held crystals and dragons,
totems to soothe me when the driving went late.
I had no choice when I built that cabin,
there in the bed of a woody wagon.

Witness statement: Luanne Cross, Red Tin neighbor

That girl deserved better than what she got.
I really can't tell you very much about Thomas —
but I curse him for wasting her sweet fierce promise.
That girl deserved better than what she got.

Thomas Kearne

I believe all museum visitors should wear black robes
and dress their hair neatly;

I believe ancient plazas should be emptied of tourists
twice a day;

I believe seats in concert halls should have a forehead rest
so that people can close their eyes and *have* the music;

I believe snowy hills should not be made to endure figures
clothed in tiger stripes and neon;

I believe only a handful of people at a time should
wander earth's sacred spaces;

I believe artists were made to save all the blessings of
nature and all the true monuments of humanity.

Birget Møller-Baeza

Last week before we drove east
I went searching for that version of Barbara Allen
where he sings it "Barbry" with just the right croakiness –
the same record I heard every few days last winter
driving to the editing bay, dodging sleet,
styrofoam morning sickness cup
revolving gently in the passenger seat:

All this while the college station earnestly kept faith with the past,
and the car's sturdy heater warmed my ankles and
steamed the windows, making for me a little cave.

Months later, I'd sit propped against the wall in the closet nursery,
the baby's shuddering breaths easing to sighs against my neck.
She didn't mind my nonsense words,
the huge gaps in my mental jukebox
In a purple aubergine
there was a sweet elf dwelling,
and so the rose grew 'round the briar
and then maybe I threw in
something about buttons,
even though that was probably from some other folk song,
some other radio.

What matters now is being out of the sleet
in this new cave,
the cats' shadows flashing through the bottom of the door,
the hinges on the woodstove top creaking,
safe safe safe,
and she and I twined together
like the rose and like the briar.

Witness statement: Katherine Kearne, mother of Thomas Kearne

I really don't want to talk about Thomas.
No one can ever know the real story.
You'll just reduce it to grim allegory.
I really don't want to talk about Thomas.

Alex Baeza

A cap of chestnut curls, Birget
murmurs at some point during the
long drive back from the Kearne filming.
Hmmmm, I say, going hand-over-hand
on the Taconic roundabout.
She comes fully awake, blinking —
She reminded me of a girl
out of American kids' books,
some Nancy Drew friend: "She tossed her
sleek cap of gleaming chestnut curls."
And him! with that golden halo!
I can tell Birget's caught up in
the coils, grasping with her greedy
editor's mind the images
of their springy hair, dark and light,
twisting together as they bent
their heads over some galley proofs.
I think about larger gyres —
of the peaked studio itself,
in a way, and, within that shape,
the bends and twists that their figures
make as they perch behind Thomas'
vast drafting table, wedged between our
cameras and the light stand, pivoting on
stools to correct
each other on obscure points of
chronology and eccentric
details from their earliest days.
Or the great and small loops Thomas
creates, spinning around the fixed
point of Delphine, first to the shelves
where he keeps local field guides, then
over to small desks and tea carts
bristling with his pencils, paints and
strange old tools, then picking his way
over our own coiled debris
to show a note from a young fan.

But if their tales that we record
are another kind of spiral
(stories of life alone on their
few acres; of "commuting" from
home triangle to work triangle
by way of the connecting shed;
their largely unsuccessful bids
to raise geese and grow strawberries;
the comedy of Delphine's first
attempt at paddling the daunting
Seven Carries canoe system)
that same horn of plenty narrows
abruptly when we ask for more.
Delphine seems willing to describe
her hometown, but beyond that she'll
share little of her murky past,
just that she fled while a minor.
Stone faced, Delphine says, *I had my*
reasons and I had my angels.
And while Thomas wants to narrate
his favorite mountain trails for
birding, and the nature of light
on the lee side of a small bay
at dusk after rain, he goes still
when we ask on background about
their cabin's official owner,
or why they've really been denied
permission to build the goose pond.
(Birget, logging the raw footage
yesterday with sound dialed back
to appease the fretful baby
realizes just how rigid
Thomas goes during this brief part
of the sit-down interview: his
shoulders pull in, his nostrils pinch.
And how, when those questions end, an
invisible bellows begins
to expand his chest cavity,
to straighten and ease his hunched spine.)
Delphine sends us up the spiral
staircase, toward the peak of the

A, where she spends much of her time
typing at the apple-green desk
with hand-turned legs – although sometimes
on rainy days, she'll move over
to the rocker with a notebook,
peering out a narrow window.
I dutifully pan around the
pale room; chase its silvery light.
Back on the lower floor, we see
that the kitchen had been gutted
to make room for the tableaux that
Thomas uses for his sketches.
(Another family strain, it's
been whispered over at Town Hall.)
It was here that they started their
first book, one commissioned by a
family friend branching into
corporate tie-ins to keep his
boyfriend's vanity press afloat;
it was here they'd first set up a
small flag and a fan, to keep the
fabric snapping just right all day,
for Thomas to sketch by the hour.

Harry Ange

At first it was just a new hobby of Marc's –
he'd always wanted to start his own small press.
It seemed pretty harmless – just one of his larks –
but then when his losses became such a mess
and he got in deep with those goddamn loan sharks –
I took a commission — *much* to his distress —
for kids' books to sell in a retail chain's stores.
Et voilà! Enter the Kearnes, through that very door.

THE BOY-SIZED FLAG

BY DELPHINE KEARNE ; ILLUSTRATED BY THOMAS KEARNE ·
ORIGINAL RELEASE DATE: MAY 1, 1973

Remember, though, that this was only supposed to be some unassuming gift shop picture book. Remember that he couldn't indulge in his skies painted like bruises, or tree knots morphing into nightmare faces. Remember she wasn't free to capture the feeling, in her bald and spare prose, of squirreling oneself away as the monsters pass by, holding one's knees, shuddering. No, this is its own animal. Pictures and story like spilled puddles of acrylic, all bright glints and parade color, with brief interludes of wistful pastels and dreamy text: *The boy-sized flag, set carefully in its playhouse bracket, felt a deft finger poke at its seventh star, then heard the breath of a question: Are you a flying sort or a planted sort?* But there are hints of them. There are hints. The dejection of the boy's figure as his little flag is carried away by a playful zephyr. (No one else could have made such an eloquent back.) And the crescent of UN flags at dusk, the poles strung like a white beaded curtain topped with misty banners. Then the clarion of the morning as the little flag wakes in a rooftop hawk's nest, its elders below, newly vibrant. (And, further still, a tiny wistful figure on the plaza grounds, suggestive of the left-behind boy.)

Witness statement: Marc Brecknell, Owner, Heartsease & Rue Press

No one can ever know the real story.
I joked to her, 'Why did you come North, fair lass?
*And how did you come to **this** pretty pass?'*
No one can ever know the whole story.

Delphine Kearne [reading from journal]

He tells me that the girl that he marries
(teasingly, as I stumble through my first portage)
will have to conquer the whole Seven Carries;

That she can't be running away with the fairies,
but stay firmly with him, bundling the cordage.
He's speaking, remember, of the girl that he marries.

When the canteen tastes of iodine and berries
and free-running streams fall to a keen shortage,
she'll have to conquer the whole Seven Carries.

(One night at a wine bar north of Kingsbury
he frowned when I laughed over paying for corkage —
not something he wants in a girl that he marries.)

I've got paddling books from the library;
I'm learning about the sins of keel warpage.
Soon he'll trust I can conquer the whole Seven Carries.

I try campfire tricks with franks and Pillsbury;
practice roping high branches for bear-proof storage.
Because he keeps saying that the girl he marries
will have to conquer the whole Seven Carries.

Harry Ange

Reader, he married her, and a good thing, too –
or so we all thought when we first met the pair.
Mind – we weren't seeing them as we all *now* do –
we just burned to enter that sales stratosphere.
Later, when the monsters came for him, I *knew*
that we'd played into the whole sorry affair.
… Now that I'm failing, I'm consumed with regret –
and fear I haven't done enough for her yet.

'Why did you come North, fair lass?'
I overheard someone say.
Well, the girl at my 4-top almost fainted away!
Why did you come North, fair lass?

Alex Baeza

What really brings her North, she says
(less on guard the next time we film)
is the whispered memory from
a dentist office magazine
opening in her listless hands
to endless, slickly-crisp pages
promoting the Adirondacks.
It feels like another country
(*The pine-tree dreameth of the palm,*
  as the palm-tree yearns for the pine)
this glimpse of deep traditions, of
one family's yearly picnic
in a small wildflower meadow
described as being located
at the far edge of their Great Camp —
how they bring the feast on horseback,
crossing streams, tremulous droplets
landing at viewer-eye level
while a blurry background figure
turns to silhouette in high sun,
hair a fluffed black dandelion.
Then they reach the pine-flanked clearing —
no sand fleas, no burrs, no flattened
frogs splayed out on hot chipped pavement —
just a rustic summer kitchen
near an oak table covered in
Indian prints, platters holding
grilled pike basted in rhubarb sauce,
sliced tomatoes, coleslaw, beer bread,
baked beans and hard apple cider ....
Somehow those few pages survive
the detritus of her teeming,
southern, middle school mind, and so
when, a handful of years later,
as that red low fog first sets in,
those magazine pages swim up –
dreamy words and vivid photos,
hand-lettered watercolor maps

of the main lodge on its own lake,
and the dozen weathered cabins
perching within the wooded hills,
and all of this surrounded by
by a miles-long oval dirt road.
So when Delphine makes that escape
from her rust-haze of pain and loss,
she holds that tall halo'd figure
in her mind, and at rest stops dreams
of hoofs effortlessly splitting
rocky eddies in rushing streams,
and wakes to thoughts of the brown squares
and the green triangles marking
all of those cabins and forests
like a child's secret treasure map.
The evasive drive North takes weeks,
the stealthy wagon keeping her
hidden and cradled at rest stops;
she spies on passing families
through the chinks in her makeshift walls.
But when the roads begin to climb
and she sees northern mountains loom,
and feels her first cold July night,
Delphine's momentum sputters out.
She gets a room at a main street
motel with thin aqua carpets
and wicker chairs in the lobby.
She showers and explores the town;
ponders the gritty alchemy
of her first Dusty Road sundae;
buys a used birdwatching field guide;
takes careful notice of a rare
24-hour coin laundromat.
And so, on the night that she plans
to leave town and head off – somewhere –
she fatefully drives the few blocks
over to the laundromat,
and, sorting through clothes in the back
of her woody wagon/cabin,
Delphine first spots Thomas inside,
slumped on a molded orange seat.

And when she crosses the threshold
and Thomas first sees her, he gapes,
looking upward at her as if
she were the exotic one, the
salvation from a certain kind
of rank small-town suffocation.
So it's only later, when he
brings her to stay in his dear house
in the pines, that she realizes
that Thomas is the same halo'd
dark figure from the magazine,
that *he* painted the treasure map,
and that *his* two-triangle home was
the one held so long in her mind.
(Does the cabin still pine for the
fifth wheel in sleep, and will the fifth
wheel see the same cabin in dreams?)

Thomas Kearne

Because peacocks belled around her ankles when she first walked
into that dingy place;

Because I saw gold slither out of her fist when she skimmed her
hands along the folding tables;

Because she made me orange pekoe tea in the back of her car with
a cigarette-lighter kettle;

Because she took my chin and nudged me to peer through a gap
in the blue plastic crates she used for walls;

Because she stilled my unreliable mind as we watched the watery
light spill from the laundromat, and the blank figures moving
between machines, billowing and taming cloth.

Birget Møller-Baeza

I winced at the jutting latex in my mouth —
not from jaw strain, but because
my mild shoulder hitch brought
the sharp bite of cat pee wafting up.

It must have been my hasty sweater
plucked from the couch.
Another wrong choice, the easy way out,
a familiar slattern shame.

Then my moue of apologetic gag
dislodged the hygienist's hand,
and I saw that her glove was the source;
caught the purple sheath's
powdered-chemical scent.

But: This jab of alarm never quite leaves,
the fear of something animal from me and mine,
seeping out, revealed.

Sometimes walking past
juniper shrubs in the medical center lot,
or a churning breakroom microwave,

I run a furtive sleeve under my nose until
it finally comes to me that I'm only smelling the orderly world;
that I won't turn a corner and find crowds
armed with pointing, sterile fingers.

Witness statement: Jasper Smith, Town Engineer

I overheard someone say
when they came walking in here hand-in-hand,
that his parents hated the pond that they'd planned.
I overheard someone say.

Alex Baeza

OK, so – cut to: Now it's four
or five books later, and now they've
had their first years of making big
splashes in small kiddie-lit ponds.
And now they're getting the bigger
contracts and the tighter deadlines –
but find themselves out of ideas.
So they scour antique stores and
find scraps of haunted wallpaper
and a costume trunk, one with a
vaguely vaudevillian aura,
for their shadowy vision of
show business props coming to life.
They bring it to their studio,
set it on its end, and slowly
pull the battered door toward them.
The interior's lined with a
watery green silk, slightly ripped.
An iron rod, still dangling some
cedar hangers, stretches across
the left-hand side of the steamer,
with the right one taken up by
three sturdy drawers, mostly empty,
but one revealing a pair of
rhinestone-encrusted tap shoes.
Then the story comes to Delphine,
fully-formed, and they start their work
of making the fantastic real.
Thomas now constructs a chest-high,
three-sided room with sloped ceiling,
and sets it up behind the trunk.
They take the old wallpaper rolls
(faded prints with peacock feathers
and fruiting vines) and glue them to
the particle-board model room,
conjuring a story about
a forgotten trunk long stored in
some out-of-the way dressing room

in an old dinner theater.
Under rare lunar cycles it
becomes a queer enchanted place:
the drawers would slowly begin
to open as the moonlight fell
through the window, the Kearnes decide.
And soon the wallpaper colors,
the trunk's pale silk lining, and the
emerging shoes themselves would be
gaining life as the lemony
spotlight spills slowly across the
faded, forgotten gabled room.
...As if they, too, are now feeling
the sweet tug of their paper moon,
Delphine and Thomas slip over
to the studio well before
sunrise each day, fully absorbed.
And it's only in the moon peace
of their creation, she now sees –
now understands – that she has been
holding her breath the last few months.
And finally the day comes when
they send in their final pages,
dismantle the particle board,
and move the antique trunk into
a corner to store art supplies.
Not long after, Thomas begins
muttering about the ski lift
once again, and its encroachment
on their circle of protection.

Delphine Kearne

Our happiest days were spent thinking of shoes —
ballet slippers, split-sole taps, and worn cowboy boots.
And he sketched by the hour, the washed greens and blues.

You'd think that their stories would be easy to choose.
They'd be married, or twins, or thieves in cahoots.
Our happiest days were spent thinking of shoes.

We didn't mind lost time; it was our time to lose,
to spin wallpaper stories of peacocks and fruits.
And he sketched by the hour, the washed greens and blues.

Then we plotted the Oz-turn, a burst of chartreuse,
faded vines slowly sprouting lurid red shoots.
Our happiest days were spent thinking of shoes.

Soon enough, each pair began dropping more clues —
little hints of backstory, with us in pursuit.
And he sketched by the hour, the washed greens and blues.

Finally story joined image, our usual fuse
of last minute magic and rude absolutes.
Then came the book of our beautiful shoes.
And after, the bruises, the washed greens and blues.

THEY'VE HUNG A STAR

BY DELPHINE KEARNE ; ILLUSTRATED BY THOMAS KEARNE ·
ORIGINAL RELEASE DATE: OCTOBER 12, 1978

But what will perhaps most be remembered by young readers is the section with no text at all, just a progressive sweep of light across the dark room, page after page, slowly transforming the icy colors of faded life into a living world, where the dressing room walls begin to bloom with flowers and birds. A standing, scuffed trunk with an abandoned wizard's cap on top becomes a little house with a peaked roof, its door swinging open. And the sleepy figures who emerge from the drawers with each turn of the page and crawl of the moonbeam also become increasingly real. O enchanted footwear: the amiable red cowboy brothers and their studded grins; the bickering old tapshoe couple, buckles snapping; the coquettish ballet slippers with ribbony tresses. And once the light finds its final spot on a black satin hatbox in the corner, each pair gets its precious time on the little stage, performing Delphine Kearne's poignant lyrics: a plaintive country tune, then a showbizzy homage, and finally, a song like a minuet filled with leaping, spinning refrains. And we're spared the grim spectre of the figures being shut away again, with the gentle final page only showing them gathered in gratitude for one more "quick bright turn" before slumber.

Part Two

But in her dreams he stands before her,
She pleads and cries and kisses his hands,
And calls him by name,
And, calling, she wakes, wakes and lies startled.
                                    —*Heinrich Heine*

Alex Baeza

The ski lift's lines are sizzling
with dark energy, Thomas claims.
He's beginning to act strangely
whenever he goes into town,
worried that the diner owner
is trying to poison Delphine;
that out-of-season fishermen
are mercenaries stalking her;
and, the biggest suspect of all:
that something is happening with
the ski resort renovations.
He swears that sometimes he can see
glints of light, probably from spy glass,
coming from up near the main lodge,
always pointed toward their cabins,
and that someone must be riding,
riding endlessly, on the lift,
keeping them under surveillance.
And often, during these last days,
she takes her coat and the string bag
from their orderly wooden pegs
on her way to the market, but
he rips them from her, grips her wrists,
holding them tighter each morning
(even as she pretends it's a game,
and brings their tangled hands up to
her mouth, kissing his whitened palms)
until she's promised to wait so
he can go with her to make sure
the agents won't snatch her away,
back to Red Tin, or somewhere else,
some horrid place he can barely
conceive, but still knows in his bones.

Witness statement: Marge Dorset, Owner, In Case of Rainy Days

They came walking in here hand-in-hand,
but from the way she was looking around
I could see she wanted to go to ground —
though they came walking in here hand-in-hand.

Harry Ange

Now, don't tell Marc, she whispered into the phone,
but there's a women's shelter hiding in town.
Wait, don't freak out on me here – *I* know that tone.
Just saying it's secret – don't spread it around. Keep
on being – Harry! – my special drop zone – for
rumors and gossip and every meltdown.
So *as* my safe house, remember your mission —
Please wave away every last dark suspicion.

Delphine Kearne

The sign above the awning read In Case of Rainy Days,
combination general store and hack tourist shop.
The meaning of the name was hiding slantways.

Thomas used to call it ol' trainy haze –
the inside sprawled like a crazed whistlestop.
The sign above the awning read In Case of Rainy Days.

It seemed to cater to every type of malaise,
with puzzles and fudge and horehound cough drops.
The meaning of the name was hiding slantways.

Have you been hearing about Marge's castaways,
Sabrina asked that day we hiked the trail's lollipop.
She told me the truth about In Case of Rainy Days.

You know that storeroom near the jars of mayonnaise –
how the door's always blocked off with a bucket and mop?
The meaning of the name was hiding slantways.

I know you'd never need it, but, well, anyways ….
Believe me, it's safer than calling a cop.
I saw then why it was called In Case of Rainy Days,
the meaning of the name emerging slantways.

He's planted the pipe bomb on a
blue ski lift chair, chained securely.
He owns his own skis, of course, but
rents some gear at the lodge to get
a feel for the relationship
of the outbuildings to the lift.
He knows that the night watchman's hut
is still on the other side of
Mount Macron — a happy fact that
allows him to destroy the spy
apparatus without killing
or even harming anyone.
(Especially "the innocents.")
After the sun goes down, there's still
one last night ride up the mountain,
one last hour skiing under lights –
his best chance for leaving the zipped
duffle behind him without it
being found and then trustingly
walked over to Security.
Does he panic, or know regret
when his skis touch the gritty snow;
when his great work ascends back up
the hill with the duffle straps wrapped
three times around the handgrip bar?
I've never really asked him that,
and all we know for sure about
his state of mind comes from those first
early days, when he keeps telling
the federal investigators
and the psychiatric doctors
that he's just very sorry, but
it all had to be done to keep
kidnappers from snatching Delphine.
When they send me the court transcripts
I think about that last film day.
He sees me hanging out of the
open passenger side window

54

as Birget slowly drives, grabbing
B-roll of the A-frame cabins.
Wait, were you filming this just now?
Did you show the outside? he asks
sharply before I even have
the chance to get out of the Jeep.
Don't use that. They're looking for her.
Delphine is leaning against a
tree, kicking backward at the trunk,
and keeps yanking her sleeves down, hard.
She throws up her hands: "Thomas!" but
then says nothing more, still keeping
the jersey's fabric wrapped and tucked
tightly between thumb and pointer.
Later, looking at logs I see
that this last interview happens
the same week Delphine goes into
the trading post, alone, and asks
more about the secret storeroom;
asks whether it's still true about
the ride to Maine, and whether the
rumored halfway house still exists.
And also if safe harbor could
be granted to someone like her,
a wife burdened only by a
man who is worried about her:
Abrupt questions that would have seemed,
I would guess, strange to anyone
but the ladies there who staff the
trading post's underground rescue.

Witness statement: Burton Trelling, Halfway House Manager

From the way she was looking around
I knew I was looking at a half of a whole.
But I could see that her heart still held a live coal,
from the way she was looking around.

Thomas Kearne

First carry really a ghost trail — that missing portage from a burned hotel;

Second carry half a mile up a slope, tough when carrying a canoe,
at the end when you can barely see, there's a narrow boardwalk;

Third carry goes to the green green water so easy, like a cool hand
on the forehead after that earlier hard haul;

Fourth carry harder to find and a little slopey, but not very long;

Fifth carry almost exactly the same as the fourth. Stone wall;

Sixth carry sweet sweet sweet, a downhill trail so short you see
the next water sparkling below as soon as you get out of the canoe.
And then when you get to that glint, it's a perfect,
miniature lake filled with soft-colored lilies, surrounded
by ferns and pines;

Seventh carry brief but sad, takes you away from the enchanted
pink and yellow circle and toward the howling, choppy waters
of Upper St. Regis   I'm not here I'm not here

Birget Møller-Baeza

Over the bassinet and out the window
came bristly small things, then orangutans and giraffes,
stomping primevally up the gravel driveway before scattering,
fading into the cottonwoods behind the house.

I tried to joke about it some mornings.
"My brain's gone all wrong," I'd drawl,
my palms pivoting on the windowsill.

But the last word dragged out, not comically,
but a lunatic gong,
wrooooooong
And I couldn't stop peering through the screening brush.

One morning I heard an elephant's strangled trumpet
and the treetops begin to shimmer —
I heard the faint screams of humans.

I was awake, I was surely awake,
but the sound came again, a monster's cry.
Then a hot air balloon breached the closest mesa,
braying air and filling the sky,
glorious and grotesque:

How it was so suddenly *there*,
an assault of color and shriek.
Like that birthing room shock, the surreal trick —
a woman splits in two, then holds herself in her arms.

Delphine Kearne

Chestnuts would come bounding across the snow to greet you
Harry's latest postcard said.
If only I had a car to come meet you.

This boarding house stinks of creeping mildew
and I climb the stairs with a rising dread.
Chestnuts would come bounding across the snow to greet you.

I've lost any home that I could retreat to.
But like a spell to chase bolting again from my head:
If only I had a car to come meet you.

We'd drive to a town like a Dickens' street view,
and I'd whistle at carts painted gold and deep red.
Chestnuts would come bounding across the snow to greet you.

His scrawled words start to seep like a bleedthrough
over the newsprint-grey from my latest med:
If only I had a car to come meet you.

Your world's gone all wrong, and I'd like to see you
if only these pills didn't pin me to bed.
Chestnuts would come bounding across the snow to greet you,
if only I had a car to come meet you.

Alex Baeza

Unbelievably, PBS
plans to carry on with the doc –
sends us funding for more travel,
assigns a producer just to
smooth the way for us (me) to get
more footage plus commentary
from new witnesses and from the
two main subjects of RLF.
But *as* to Thomas and Delphine –
these new interviews are a strain,
and though they're of course conducted
separately, they feel like joint –
each of them speaking as if trapped
underwater, and odder still,
though they're hundreds of miles apart,
each eerily seeming to start
right where the other one leaves off –
even with contact between them
forbidden by the legal terms
that keep Thomas out of prison
and in a state-run hospital,
and save Delphine from being charged.
That threat is one last bruise for her,
I'm sure, remembering how she
couldn't stop tugging down her sleeves
the final day of interviews.
I have herbal tea with Thomas
in the psych ward's solarium,
then drive seven hours to walk on
rocky seaside piers with Delphine.
She refuses to share details
of her two days waiting in the
storeroom until the van came late
one night to bring her here to Maine.
She thinks there might be some money
after paying Thomas' lawyers
(but noted grimly that soon his
parents might sell some property

to settle the ski lodge's suit).
For now, though, she's working on some
ghostwriting that Harry Ange has
conjured up from an old contact;
she writes grade school content about
global holiday traditions.
Harry's also arranged from his
sickbed for a typewriter and
for a small bi-weekly stipend –
and, ever the fixer, also
urged Birget and me to take her
to dinner; to buy her new clothes.
I don't tell him that the darkness
is now stalking our own home, or
about Birget's constant nightmares –
whether they're just postpartum or
the shock of the bombing, or both,
I cannot say, or even guess.

DK   sheets smelling of cream,
a tabletop jade fountain —
my only fixed points of rest

TK   a man ushers me
from bed to shower each day,
one hand bangelingling my wrist

             ~

DK   on a snowy night
a bag boy's mercy moves me —
the strength of doubled plastic

TK   the crackle of sleet
hitting cellophane-sheathed books;
a librarian's tired smile

             ~

DK   I dump the ashtray
in the toilet down the hall,
twist the shower taps open

TK   ropes of water fall
on my unworthy shoulders:
benediction. that soft grace

DK   four silver barrettes
clipped to my last elastic,
like a warden's keyring

TK   garden chores now done,
I form tiny chickweed wreaths;
marvel at the tensile coils

DK   boarders slyly drop
guilty bottles from the roof,
chiming in the first warm nights

TK   sudden squeaks on rubber
as the late shift make their rounds;
bedsprings answer fretfully

DK   night air turns softer,
basil grows on the wide sill;
Evensong sieves through the screen

TK   on my way back from
church service one soft night
frogs snap out like rubber bands

Harry Ange

Yes, I do what I can to keep her going –
until she's ready for real work again.
It's not much – but it keeps contacts flowing.
And hell, I even check on *him* when I can –
a *most* unpleasant task, even when knowing
how a disease like that could take down a man.
But I must tell you – I find it unnerving –
their minds are still linked – it's just quite disturbing.

Witness statement: Sylvie Newman, Thomas Kearne's case worker

I knew I was looking at half of the whole.
But he needs to find his own true stillness.
(It's not just feeding them pills for their illness.)
I knew I was looking at half of the whole.

Alex Baeza

Sometimes I feel like half my life
is spent in talking to doctors –
my family's and my subjects'.
But that's …. I don't really know,
as I talk into this and watch
the ribbon slither off the left
spool before circling the right one,
exactly how much I'm going
to even use of all this stuff.
Grim, grim, grim joke that my partner
would know what to cut, what to leave;
how much of *us* to keep in here,
or even whether to keep on
with Thomas and Delphine at all.
For now, though, the project's still on.
Ya gotta line up, Baeza.
Status: it's now early summer,
and I'm told Thomas and Delphine,
again so eerily in tune,
are starting to show hopeful signs
according to their case workers.
Thomas has been working with a
master herbalist, or something,
one who comes to the hospital
and takes walks with him on the grounds,
pointing out the most healing plants.
He's learning to make mystic baths.
That's a thing, they tell me, where you
meditate on your intentions,
or on the person you're making
the bath for, and then go out to
gather the right herbs and flowers
that came into your reverie
earlier. And *then* you steep them
for a long solemn interval,
finally straining the infused
waters into a waiting bath.
(More importantly, to my mind,

and to those who deserve to know,
he's not resisting his real meds.)
Delphine is slowly regaining
her old faith in working alone;
she's been reading some history
between all her freelancing gigs.
And both of them, their doctors say,
understand their time together
is now done, court-ordered or not.
And each of them works toward peace,
or toward some pale version of peace.

He needs to find his own true stillness.
But there's something about that ribbon of light;
I can sense it in him — it will soon pull him right.
He needs to find his own true stillness.

Thomas Kearne

Dear heart, on the sacred days in other parts of the world, I sneak
out to the warm waters and commune with you and whatever
goddesses of forgiveness I can conjure;

Dear heart, on the night of Peille Fête boys give their sweethearts
"flowering apples" – oranges stuffed with blooms. I preserve
rose petals, shape them into a maroon sphere that dries hard as wood, then
roll its tacky surface in grated peel;

Dear heart, when New Year for the Trees happens the four wines are
poured solemnly over fifteen separate fruits. I eat one each day until only
liquid stays, then boil the infusion to paste;

Dear heart, a clear pitcher is filled with fresh-picked white flowers to start
the Waters of Oxalá celebration. I run spring water over fresh mountain
laurel, then place the jug in a green cupboard;

Dear heart, an egg gets hollowed, then stuffed with five bay leaves and salt,
for Lovers' Divination. I crush the filled egg, write *Delphine* on paper strips,
knead this mixture together with river clay and dry it in the sun;

Dear heart, *Crack and pull out,* they say before Palestine Easter.
What is the remedy for the head? These words call forth love. I cut
sweet herbs as I chant, then place the bowl under the stars;

Dear heart, each St. John's Day brings fig-eating expeditions,
and the testing of true love. Do torn fig leaves heal? Will the artichokes
flower? And does the spun needle float?;

Dear heart, had you never driven up in your wood-paneled car I
would not have known the roundness, the warm mellow note, that can
cushion this cold, thin air, even now;

Dear heart, if I paint again the shortest brush strokes will be breaths of
memory — the glints of red in your hair and the cedar dock as you rose on
your toes, poised to dive;

Dear heart, the longer, deeper marks will be the shame of when I dared to
bind your spirit to mine, before the welts on your wrists finally changed
from wine to pale green.

Birget Møller-Baeza

I keep vigil for my little sister –
put off her visit as long as possible, true, but still I keep vigil:
Keep sheets clean and waiting in the cupboard;
freeze vegetarian dinners and extra breastmilk; send out invoices.

It's kind of weird to call it a sister, I grumble to my therapist,
pinning a thumbnail's half-moon into my palm.
Just try it, she says. Get things ready.
But organizing is full of minefields –
I keep finding my old flimsy shields, guarding ghosts.

The hat boxes stacked into steps near the bed should be put away
but I can still feel the warm sides of the blind cat
patiently letting me guide him,
his loyal heart beating between my two palms
as his claws scrabbled across the slick surface.

The squat plastic jars hang pointlessly
from the vegetable garden fence,
their clear sides showing cotton balls yellowed
with the futile hue of bottled coyote urine.

A clothesline sags between the trees at the back border,
ragged shreds of black plastic bags still attached at the top.
(I once earnestly believed the pamphlet promising that
guinea hens would be too scared to cross under the rustle.)

There's a tiny gray cabin near the base of one of the hills I climb,
fronted by a pair of green lawn chairs.
The first day I went by – two years ago now –
I saw a navy blue cardigan draped girlishly
over the back of the chair nearest the path.
I cut my eyes straight so I wouldn't disturb its owner
when she came back out the screen door.
But the door never opened, and
the sweater's been there ever since, growing paler each month,
the plastic edges of the lawn chairs fraying into neon curls.

Will Alex, if I finally lose my way, all the way,
feel compelled to keep the dead cat's stairs by the bed,
to leave out the totems protecting long-gone guineas
and abducted seedlings?
Would he leave my boots to keep vigil
from their square of newspaper on the front porch?

We're a team, he reminds me.
But lately when I think about true artistic partnerships
I don't think of Delphine and Thomas, their ruins.
I don't flash back to soundchecks with Alex,
or his hands on the wheel, knuckles white with forced affability.

I think of that invented baby sister,
the depressive other half I'm supposed to picture tenderly.
I yearn for her with the ache of withheld sleep.
Next time when I feel her coming,
I will lift the covers for her, draw her in,
and we will dream our dreams together.

New Biography Joins Regional Small Press Spring Roundup

March 10, 1981

Glens Falls-based publisher Heartsease & Rue Press is launching its nonfiction division with the release of *We Will Not Die, They Whisper*, by first-time author Darcy Megget. The biography examines the life of Opal Stanley Whiteley, a remarkable American writer who entered public notice with the audacious claim that her true father was Prince Henri of Orleans, France — but who tragically died, long-forgotten, in the London asylum where she'd been a patient for decades.

Accounts regarding Whiteley's early life differ between her own insistence that she was raised in a lumber camp as the abandoned daughter of Prince Henri, and those of her presumably legitimate relatives, who say she had a conventional childhood living with her biological family.

"Wherever she really came from, what we do know for sure is that at a young age she left a home that she alleged was abusive," Megget explained. Whiteley began earning money as a writer while still a young woman, and soon became a sensation with 1920's *The Story of Opal*, which her publisher presented as Whitely's childhood diary.

Those who know her work well universally agree that Whiteley should be much better known.

Readers will now also have the chance to view substantial excerpts of *The Fairy land Around Us*. (This was the manuscript Whiteley originally sought to publish, before a publisher suggested that if she could in fact produce the childhood diaries she was quoting during meetings, it might better fit in with the public's then-fascination with uncanny children.)

Of researching and writing the story of Whiteley's life, Megget said, "It probably goes without saying for any biographer anyway, but it was a challenge to clear up the disparity between what Opal claimed about herself (perhaps with the motive of self-protection), what the people marketing her books said to drum up interest — and reality itself, at least as we would see it in our modern age.

"I'm also grateful that several avid collectors gave me their blessing to look at many elusive documents and manuscripts for this project," added Megget.

[VO] Witness statement: Fan letter to the Kearnes from Daniel L, 12

There's something about the ribbon of light
falling on the trunk in that forgotten back room.
Sometimes when I can't get away from my gloom
I open your books for that ribbon of light.

Notes on the characters and their poetic forms

Each interviewed character or entity in this fictional documentary transcript speaks in their own specific poetic form.

Alex Baeza - Blank Verse
Alex Baeza, as director and narrator of the documentary about Delphine and Thomas Kearne, is also the main narrator of this collection. He speaks in classic narrative or blank verse (specifically, iambic tetrameter).

Delphine Kearne - Villanelle
The villanelle, a French poem dating from the Renaissance period, is lyrical, draped around a strong armature, and (with its idiosyncratic repeating lines and rhyme scheme) a little unpredictable – all traits true of Delphine herself.

Thomas Kearne -Anaphora
Thomas' interviews are conducted in anaphora. Even at the time he meets Delphine, he is beginning to struggle with looping thoughts and emphatic opinions, underlined by the repetitive nature of anaphora.

Delphine and Thomas - Sedoka
Ancient sedoka poems from Japan consisted of two, 3-line stanzas (katuata) with a 5-7-7 / 5-7-7 syllable structure. Usually the first katuata was written by one of a pair of lovers, and the other lover answered in the second katuata. The two cycles of Delphine and Thomas' sedoka take place, respectively, before and after their time together, but always serve to intuitively echo one another's thoughts.

Harry Ange - Ottava Rima
The eight-line stanza form known as the ottava rima is the voice given to Harry Ange, the courtly editor of Delphine and Thomas' books. He later acts as something of a mentor and lifeline to Delphine. The ottava rima struck me as just playful enough, but also formal enough, to convey his fatherly attachment to Delphine.

Birget Møller-Baeza -Free Verse
Birget, the artistic and life partner making documentaries with Alex, speaks in free verse, a deceptively conversational form.

The 12 Witnesses - Catena Rondo

Because the accounts from relatives, friends and acquaintances of the couple are woven throughout this "transcript", using the catena rondo form serves as a way to connect these witness statements to one another. Created by British poet Robin Skelton as a play on the traditional rondue, this "chain" is linked by the first line and fourth line of each quatrain, repeating the second line from the one preceding it. While the dozen quatrains in this volume are not presented on consecutive pages, they are connected by the repetitive form.

Lake Tanager Community - Found Poetry

Here, the found poem tradition operates as a kind of a Greek chorus for the Adirondack town most impacted by Thomas' actions. In keeping with the sometimes taciturn Yankee mindset, their true feelings are revealed secondhand, by what they choose to highlight in therapeutic multimedia pieces featuring news clippings about Delphine and Thomas.

The Books - Ekphrasis

The Kearne's first and last picture books "speak" in ekphrasis (poetry that describes a specific piece of art). I chose to use the prose poem form of ekphrasis, acting a kind of heightened version of a Kirkus-type book review.

Acknowledgments

The following publications previously published selections from this collection:

The Dillydoun Review, "Because peacocks belled around her ankles"

Open: Journal of Arts and Letters, the complete sedoka interview cycles "light fell down/snow blurred" and "sheets smelling of cream/a man ushers"

Rat's Ass Review, "I had no choice but to build a cabin," "He tells me that the girl that he marries," and "Our happiest days were spent thinking of shoes"

I would like to thank the two closest, most patient readers of these poems (both individually and as a collection): My dear friend, Karen Holmberg, and my husband, Michael A. Reilly.

My children, Phoebe Jordan-Reilly and Henry Jordan-Reilly, have also provided invaluable insight over the years and continually inspire me through their own work.

I would also like to thank the late J.D. O'Hara for his profound influence, as well as for contributing the chestnuts in the snow imagery.

About the Author

Melissa E. Jordan lives in northwestern Connecticut. Her poetry collection, *Bain-Marie* (Big Wonderful Press) was published in 2015. Jordan's poems have appeared or are forthcoming *in The Cossack Review, The Dillydoun Review, Open: Journal of Art & Letters, Word Riot, Otis Nebula, Terrain, Off the Coast, Rat's Ass Review,* and elsewhere.